Snakes on the Hunt

RATTLESNAKES

Shaye Reynolds

PowerKiDS press

New York

Published in 2017 by The Rosen Publishing Group, Inc.
29 East 21st Street, New York, NY 10010

First Edition

Editor: Caitie McAneney
Book Design: Mickey Harmon

Photo Credits: Cover, pp. 1, 6, 8, 10, 14, 18, 20 (series logo) iLoveCoffeeDesign/Shutterstock.com; cover, pp. 1, 3, 4, 6, 8, 10, 12, 14, 16, 18, 20, 22—24 (background) cla78/Shutterstock.com; cover (rattlesnake), p. 7 Audrey Snider-Bell/Shutterstock.com; p. 5 Joe McDonald/Shutterstock.com; p. 9 John Cancalosi/National Geographic Magazines/Getty Images; p. 10 fivespots/Shutterstock.com; p. 11 Steve Byland/Shutterstock.com; p. 13 Ryan M. Bolton/Shutterstock.com; p. 15 Susan Schmitz/Shutterstock.com; p. 16 John Cancalosi/Photo Library/Getty Images; p. 17 Rob Roeck/Shutterstock.com; p. 19 Hiciu Catalin/Shutterstock.com; p. 20 Andrew Sabai/Shutterstock.com; p. 21 Mark Skalny/Shutterstock.com; p. 22 IrinaK/Shutterstock.com.

Cataloging-in-Publication Data

Names: Reynolds, Shaye.
Title: Rattlesnakes / Shaye Reynolds.
Description: New York : PowerKids Press, 2017. | Series: Snakes on the hunt | Includes index.
Identifiers: ISBN 9781499422023 (pbk.) | ISBN 9781499422047 (library bound) | ISBN 9781499422030 (6 pack)
Subjects: LCSH: Rattlesnakes–Juvenile literature.
Classification: LCC QL666.O69 R49 2017| DDC 597.96–dc23

Manufactured in the United States of America

CPSIA Compliance Information: Batch #BS16PK: For Further Information contact Rosen Publishing, New York, New York at 1-800-237-9932

Contents

A Warning Rattle. 4

Rattlesnake Features 6

Life of a Rattler 8

Rattlesnake Range 10

Rattlesnake Senses 12

That's a Warning! 14

Hunters and Hunted. 16

Time to Hunt! 18

Rattlesnakes and People. 20

Respect for the Rattlesnake 22

Glossary 23

Index. 24

Websites 24

A Warning Rattle

It's common knowledge in the animal world that a rattling sound means trouble. Rattlesnakes often make that sound before they strike. If you're a **rodent** or another small animal, it could be the last thing you ever hear!

There are over 20 species, or kinds, of rattlesnake. You can tell them apart by their different sizes, colors, and patterns. However, they all have a rattle on the tip of their tail. Their rattle is a **defense** against predators. It's the rattlesnake's final warning before it bites!

Rattlesnakes are venomous, which means they can deliver poison to another animal through their bite.

5

Rattlesnake Features

Adult rattlesnakes can be as short as 1 foot (0.3 m) or as long as 8 feet (2.4 m)! The longest rattlesnake in the world is the eastern diamondback rattlesnake. This snake can weigh up to 10 pounds (4.5 kg).

Rattlesnakes have a triangle-shaped head. The different patterns on their skin help them blend in with their **habitat**. Western diamondback rattlesnakes and eastern diamondback rattlesnakes both have a diamond pattern on their skin. They have two dark stripes on each side of their face.

Snake Bites

Rattlesnakes usually have dark green, brown, gray, or black skin. They shed their skin as they grow.

This western diamondback rattlesnake has black and white bands on its tail.

Life of a Rattler

Rattlesnakes are solitary animals, which means they usually live and hunt alone. However, rattlesnakes sometimes share a den. Dens can be **burrows** underground or spaces between rocks. You don't want to come across a den in the wild!

A rattlesnake mother must find a den to have her babies. Rattlesnake mothers give birth to their babies in the summertime. Unlike many snakes, rattlesnakes don't lay eggs. The babies are wrapped in a clear covering. When they break out, they're ready to hunt.

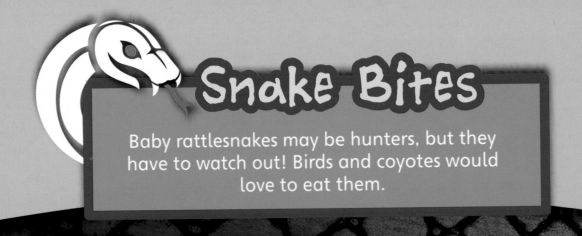

Snake Bites

Baby rattlesnakes may be hunters, but they have to watch out! Birds and coyotes would love to eat them.

Juvenile, or young, rattlesnakes have a venomous bite, too!

Rattlesnake Range

Where can you find rattlesnakes? They're found in many **regions** of North America and South America. Western diamondback rattlesnakes make their home in Arizona, New Mexico, Louisiana, California, Oklahoma, Texas, and Mexico. Eastern diamondback rattlesnakes make their home in eastern states from southern North Carolina to Florida.

Rattlesnakes live in many different habitats. They live and hunt in grasslands, woodlands, swamps, and meadows. Some are found in rocky hills or on the coast. Rattlesnakes like to be able to hide behind rocks and in grass.

Snake Bites

The Mexican west coast rattlesnake is named after its home in western Mexico.

Many rattlesnakes are found in the desert. If you're walking in the American Southwest or central Mexico, watch out for the Mojave rattlesnake!

Rattlesnake Senses

Snakes have supersenses to help them survive and hunt. Rattlesnakes have a great sense of sight, even at night. They can also feel vibrations, or small, quick movements, on the ground.

Rattlesnakes pick up smells with their tongue. Then, their tongue passes over a special body part called the Jacobson's **organ** on the roof of their mouth. This part recognizes the smell. Rattlesnakes have other special body parts called pit organs between their **nostrils** and eyes. These pits help rattlesnakes sense the temperature of objects around them.

When another animal walks by, a rattlesnake senses the animal's body heat with its pit organs.

nostril

pit organ

13

That's a Warning!

Rattlesnakes can be deadly. However, there are a few animals that dare to approach them. Luckily, the rattlesnake has a special defense—its rattle.

When a rattlesnake sees a possible predator, it shakes its rattle very quickly. The rattle is made of keratin, which is what your fingernails are made of. The hollow segments, or parts, click together to make the rattling sound. This sound tells predators that the snake is ready to attack.

Snake Bites

Each time a rattlesnake molts, or sheds its skin, a new segment forms on its rattle. The segments chip and break over time.

A rattlesnake can shake its rattle more than 60 times per second.

15

Hunters and Hunted

Rattlesnakes are one of the greatest predators in their food chain. They're known to go after lizards and even small birds that are on the ground. Rattlesnakes love to hunt small rodents, such as mice, rats, and squirrels.

Even as deadly predators, rattlesnakes have their own predators to worry about. Big birds, such as hawks and eagles, swoop down to catch rattlesnakes. King snakes are known to eat rattlesnakes, too. Coyotes and bobcats will also pick a fight with this rattling hunter.

A roadrunner catches a rattlesnake.

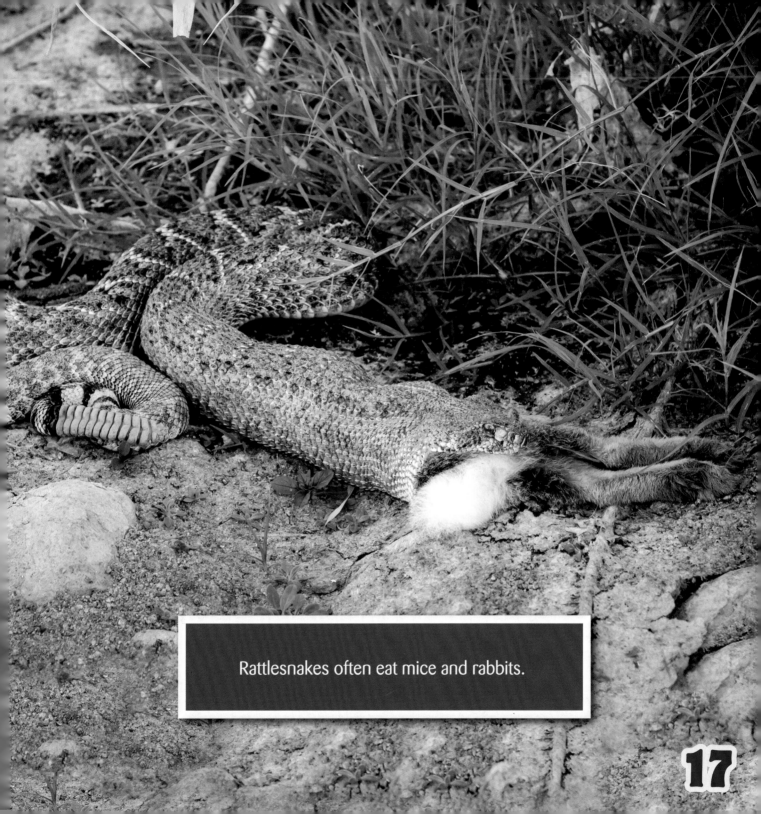

Rattlesnakes often eat mice and rabbits.

Time to Hunt!

Rattlesnakes often like to hunt at night. During the day, the snake curls up in its hiding place. By late evening, it's time to hunt. The rattlesnake leaves its den and slithers along the ground. It uses its supersenses to find and track **prey**.

When the rattlesnake finds its prey, it strikes. It sinks its fangs into the animal and delivers deadly venom. The animal might run away, but the venom will soon kill it. The rattlesnake finds the dead animal using its supersenses. Then, it's time to eat!

Snake Bites

Like most snakes, rattlesnakes can go without eating for weeks.

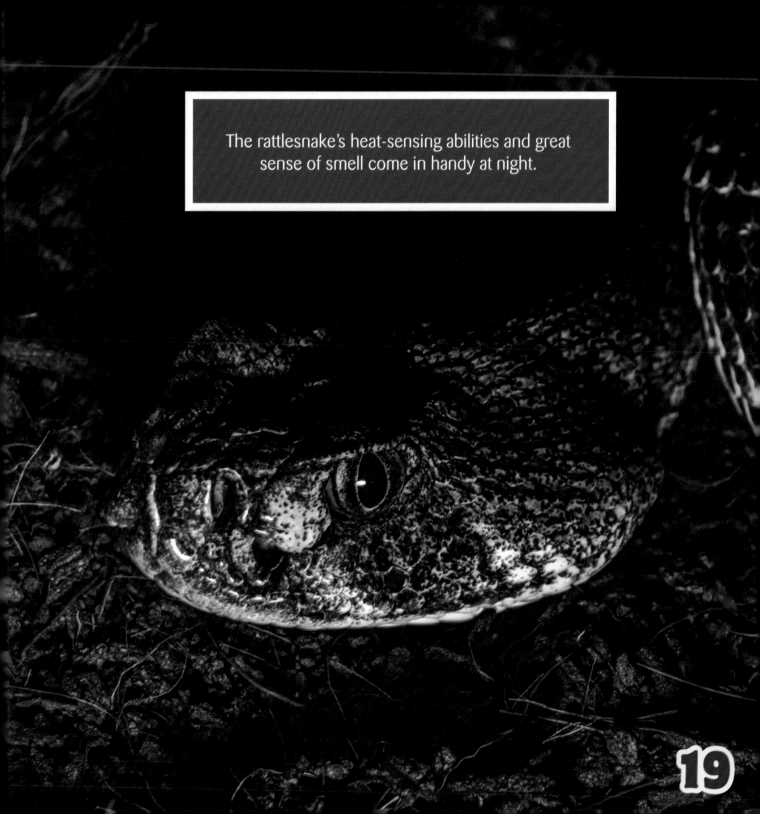

The rattlesnake's heat-sensing abilities and great sense of smell come in handy at night.

Rattlesnakes and People

People in the North American Southwest have lived alongside the rattlesnake for thousands of years. Native peoples have many stories of this snake and its deadly bite. There's a good reason to be afraid. Western diamondback rattlesnakes bite hundreds of people every year.

Luckily, rattlesnakes rarely want to hurt people. Many species aren't **aggressive** and just want to be left alone. If a rattlesnake does bite, a person can take a special drug called antivenin. This slows the venom and saves the person's life.

BEWARE
Rattlesnakes!

Snake Bites

Most rattlesnake bites happen when a person bothers a den or tries to pick up a rattlesnake.

People rarely die from rattlesnake bites, but it's important to get to the hospital right away.

Respect for the Rattlesnake

Rattlesnakes may be scary, but they're not out to hurt people. These great hunters would rather hide in the grass and track their prey. In fact, people are more of a risk to rattlesnakes. People ruin rattlesnake habitats when they cut down trees and build on once-wild land. Some people hunt rattlesnakes. People driving cars may hit rattlesnakes when the snakes cross the street.

However, this hunter deserves respect. They have a deadly bite, but we need rattlesnakes to keep **ecosystems** healthy.

Glossary

aggressive: Showing a readiness to attack.

burrow: A hole an animal digs in the ground for shelter.

defense: A feature of a living thing that helps keep it safe.

ecosystem: All the living things in an area.

habitat: The natural place where an animal or plant lives.

nostril: An opening through which an animal breathes.

organ: A body part that does a certain task.

prey: An animal hunted by other animals for food.

region: A large area of land that has a number of features in common.

rodent: A small, furry animal with large front teeth, such as a mouse or rat.

Index

B
babies, 8
birds, 8, 16
bobcats, 16

C
coyotes, 8, 16

E
eagles, 16
eastern
     diamondback
     rattlesnakes,
     6, 10

H
hawks, 16

J
Jacobson's
     organ, 12

K
king snakes, 16

L
lizards, 16

M
Mexican west coast
     rattlesnake, 10
Mexico, 10
Mojave
     rattlesnake, 11

N
New Mexico, 10
North America, 10

P
pit organ, 12, 13
predators, 4, 14, 16
prey, 18, 22

R
rats, 16
rattle, 4, 14, 15
rodent, 4, 16

S
South America, 10
species, 4, 20
squirrels, 16

T
Texas, 10

V
venom, 4, 9, 18, 20

W
western
     diamondback
     rattlesnakes, 6,
     7, 10, 20

Websites

Due to the changing nature of Internet links, PowerKids Press has developed an online list of websites related to the subject of this book. This site is updated regularly. Please use this link to access the list: www.powerkidslinks.com/soth/rattl